'Young Amazons' writing letters home during a quiet afternoon in September 1941 on a temporary balloon site.

The WAAF

A History of the Women's Auxiliary Air Force in the Second World War

Squadron Leader Beryl E. Escott

A Shire book

Contents

Cover: *Activity in RAF Kenley (Surrey) operations room during the Canadian Wing operations, 1943–4. This painting was exhibited at the Royal Academy in 1944. (Courtesy of the artist, Lilian Buchanan – a WAAF)*

ACKNOWLEDGEMENTS

Photographs and other illustrations are reproduced by courtesy of the following: Gwendoline Ayres, page 25 (bottom); Beryl Bacon, pages 13 (top), 34 (bottom two); Kathleen Baker, page 37 (bottom); Dee Ball, page 4 (bottom); Basil Beagent, page 1; Dorothy Bell, page 26 (bottom); Bletchley Park Trust, page 15 (top two); Yvonne Bottwood, page 8 (bottom); Lilian Buchanan, front cover; Helen Chappell, page 3 (bottom); Joy Cornell, page 22 (bottom); Joan Crane, page 17 (bottom); Crown Copyright/MOD, pages 3 (top), 7 (bottom), 10 (bottom two), 11 (both), 14 (top), 17 (top), 38, 39; Mrs D'Acre, page 4 (top); Marcelle Davies, page 33 (centre); Mrs De Margolese-Braz, page 24 (upper centre); *Derby Evening Telegraph*, pages 6 (bottom), 23 (top); Gwendoline Dunn, page 14 (bottom); Amy Durance, page 21 (bottom); Beryl E. Escott, pages 8 (top), 9 (top), 20 (centre), 28 (top right), 36 (top); Mrs Farrow, page 29 (bottom left); Winifred Field, page 37 (top); Vera Furneaux, page 24 (top); J. G. Gilchrist-Brown, pages 20 (both), 35 (both); Edna Gulley, page 34 (top); Gertrude Hodges, page 19 (bottom); Mrs A. Horton, page 27 (top); Delicia Iremonger, page 36 (bottom); Gwyneth James, page 12 (top); Pauline Lambert, page 25 (top); Catherine Lockey, page 33 (bottom); Elsie Miller, page 21 (top); Mrs Miller, page 7 (top); W. A. Newton, page 27 (bottom left); Lesley Nightingale, page 6 (top); Dorothy Osbon, page 9 (bottom left); Mrs A. Parsons, page 28 (top left); Valerie Pearman-Smith, page 9 (bottom right); Sylvia Pickering, page 22 (top two); Mary Potter, page 33 (top); Royal Air Force Museum, Hendon, pages 5 (top), 10 (top), 15 (bottom), 24 (bottom right), 37 (bottom); Francis Rudge, page 18 (top); R. J. Scarlett, pages 27 (bottom right), 28 (top centre), 30 (top right), 31 (top and bottom); Freddie Smith, page 13 (bottom); Hilda Smith, page 16; Joan Smith, page 20 (bottom); Special Forces Club, page 30 (bottom); Lady Stewart, page 31 (centre); Jean Stocks, page 12 (centre); Sheila Ternan, page 12 (bottom); *This England*, pages 28 (bottom), 30 (top left); Florentia Vachon, page 32; Vera Webb, page 24 (bottom left); Weidenfeld & Nicolson, page 29 (top two and bottom right).

British Library Cataloguing in Publication Data: Escott, Beryl E. The WAAF: a history of the women's Auxiliary Force in the Second World War. – (Shire album; 422) 1. Great Britain. Royal Air Force. Women's Auxiliary Air Force – History. 2. World War, 1939–1945 – Participation, Female I. Title. 940.5'44941. ISBN 0 7478 0572 5.

Published in 2007 by Shire Publications Ltd, Midland House, West Way, Botley, Oxford OX2 0PH, UK. (Website: www.shirebooks.co.uk)

Copyright © 2007 by Beryl E. Escott. First published 2003; reprinted 2008. Shire Album 422. ISBN 978 0 7478 0572 4.

Printed in Malta by Gutenberg Press Ltd, Gudja Road, Tarxien PLA 19, Malta.

Before the Second World War

WAAF predecessors, 1918–39

The Royal Air Force (RAF) and the Women's Royal Air Force (WRAF) were formed together on 1st April 1918. When the First World War broke out in 1914, planes flying at 70 mph (113 km/h) and women wearing trousers were considered fast. By 1918 things had changed. Though given no organised training, the WRAF carried out a remarkable number of jobs, from sailmakers and dopers of planes to engine fitters, while Blandford Camp was kept alight by women electricians. At its height the WRAF reached 24,659 members, and in 1919 over one thousand were serving in Germany. Nevertheless, because of economy cuts after the war the force was disbanded on 1st April 1920.

In the 1930s German rearmament caused the British Government to start desultory preparations for another possible war and some women's organisations followed suit. Most notable was the Emergency Service, which struck out on its own in October 1936 under the redoubtable Dame Helen Gwynne-Vaughan (WRAF Commandant, 1918–20). Membership entailed

Above: WRAF at work on a biplane, 1919. Notice that they are wearing dungarees for dirty work.

Winston Churchill, Minister for War, inspects the WRAF, serving with the RAF on the Rhine in Cologne in August 1919.

3

The Women's Emergency Corps drilling in the Duke of York's Buildings, London, October 1938.

training at least one evening a week, summer camps, and a fee of 10 shillings (50 pence) a year. This 'blouse and skirt army' endured social ostracism, harsh conditions and governmental disapproval, but it persevered.

In September 1938, the Munich Crisis brought forward the formation of the Auxiliary Territorial Service (ATS) to 27th September. Every British county was to raise several companies affiliated to a local (male) army Territorial unit, but one was to be a Royal Air Force ATS company, later affiliated to an Auxiliary Royal Air Force (RAF) unit. After one of their drill sessions the women staggered to their chairs, their drill sergeant commenting, 'You don't know the difference between men and women recruits. I give them the same drill and they're just as bad.' On 28th June 1939, the two services separated and the Women's

The first viewing of new uniforms for female volunteers, July 1939: (left to right) ATS; WRNS; WAAF; London Ambulance Service; Land Army.

4

Senior Controller, later Air Commandant, and after 1942 Air Chief Commandant (Dame 1944) Katherine Jane Trefusis-Forbes DBE LLD, the first WAAF Director (1939–43). In 1966 she married Sir Robert Watson-Watt.

Auxiliary Air Force (WAAF) was born. The Women's Royal Naval Service (WRNS) had appeared on 3rd April 1939.

The WAAF and its companies

The WAAF, by now 1734 strong, was headed by Katherine Trefusis-Forbes. She had been a trainee and Chief Instructor in the Emergency Service and was described by one WAAF as being 'neat as a new pin, and given to roaring to work on her motorbike'. Her WAAF members were spread over the country in forty-seven companies. Those companies attached to the Flying Squadrons were supposed to have sixty-seven women each, serving as cooks, clerks, mess orderlies, mechanical transport drivers and equipment assistants; Balloon Centres were to have five more women, as fabric workers. However, not all companies were full.

An RAF/WAAF cap badge.

5

The National Defence Rally of All Women's Services in Hyde Park, before King George VI, Queen Elizabeth and Queen Mary, on 2nd July 1939. This was the first public wearing of the WAAF uniform, four days after the force was formed.

The early years

Recruitment and mobilisation

It was the task of the WAAF companies to prepare their women to be officers or senior non-commissioned officers (SNCOs) so that there was always a core force to train future airwomen. At first WAAF volunteers were *enrolled*, being able to leave when they wished (and a few did), but by 25th April 1941 so many were involved in secret work that the **Defence (Women's Forces) Regulations** were passed, making members subject to RAF discipline and rules. In 1942 the **National Service Act** of 1941 began calling up girls born in 1920 and 1921. This move – gradually extended and eventually yielding about 33,932, frequently unwilling, WAAF – was not generally welcomed by the earlier volunteers.

Early in August 1939, the Air Ministry, which had declared it needed no WAAF

WAAF recruiting began in September 1939. Shown here is a WAAF recruiting drive in Derby, October 1941. Recruiting stopped in 1943 but resumed intermittently until 1945.

6

Most early WAAF recruits had no proper accommodation or uniform; nor did they have a clear idea of their duties or any helpful traditions to follow. In October 1939 these airwomen, in airmen's clothing, are consulting the few rules they do have, as they clean and prepare buildings on their new station.

for several months, was panicked into appealing for telephonists, teleprinter operators, plotters and radar operators for desperate RAF stations. From 25th August telegrams went out mobilising all WAAF, and on 3rd September 1939, when war was declared on Germany, recruitment began for a further 10,000 women. Immediately companies and the Air Ministry were besieged by applicants. 'Have you seen them, Madam?', a perspiring policeman asked the WAAF director. 'The queue stretches from Victory House ... almost to Whitehall!'

Volunteers came from all walks of life. They tended to be young, patriotic, glad to escape from home or job, and were occasionally nursing revenge; flying and the spirit of adventure attracted them. Many were from as far afield as the dominions, the colonies and other friendly countries. The companies (all closed by March 1940) were often forced to send untrained women straight to stations, which were themselves unprepared for the sudden influx of airmen – let alone airwomen. These stations were often only half built, with no WAAF accommodation, uniforms or proper jobs, and with unhelpful staff. 'The RAF just wasn't ready for us', bemoaned one WAAF. Such unsatisfactory conditions lasted into 1941, as the number of women recruited far exceeded the facilities available. Numbers peaked at about 182,000 in 1943, when recruiting temporarily stopped.

The training environment

Basic training for airwomen was a necessity and was soon introduced. In a largely female environment and a crammed two to three weeks, civilians were turned into airwomen. Usually the first day at reception saw them kitted out and

'WAAF Kitting Up, 1941'. This illustration shows a vast conveyor-belt system for the equipping of new recruits at RAF Innsworth, Gloucestershire. (Painting by Charles Cundall)

Wartime Moves of WAAF Depots 1939–45

	1939	1940	1941	1942	1943	1944-45
West Drayton	10	9				
Harrogate		No. 1			South Receiving & Training	
		9	5			
Innsworth			No. 2	Receiving Only	2 8	
			12	10		
Bridgnorth			No. 1			
			8	9		
Morecambe			No. 3 Training Only		2 North Receiving & Training	
			10			
Wilmslow					Receiving & Training	All. Receiving & Training
					2 8	

Diagram of the wartime moves of the WAAF Basic Training Depots.

The Passing Out Parade of WAAF trainees along the front at Morecambe Bay, Lancashire, August 1942. Note the length of the parade.

given the dreaded FFI ('free from infection)' checks – 'a quick flash, pants down and up', as one girl described it. The next day, or soon after, came tests for the allocation of trades. Girls wore uniform all the time and marched everywhere in groups ('flights') to meals, lectures on the RAF, gas, fire, first aid, hygiene and physical training, sports, injections ('like pincushions for doctors to practise on'), dental checks, pay parades and still more drill and tough discipline.

If in huts, they slept twelve to twenty-three per room, head to toe alternately, in iron beds 6 feet long and 2¹/₂ feet wide (183 by 76 cm). They had three square, fawn, buttoned, straw-filled mattresses ('biscuits'), two white cotton sheets and grey wool blankets. The bedding was to be stacked for inspection every morning and the area cleaned, with dire results if unsatisfactory. On the first night many girls wept into their straw pillows, but despite the hardship, or because of it, they learned to work and laugh together, made close friends and became resilient and adaptable. They exchanged comfort for comradeship, proud of their contribution to the men who flew. Air raids and rising numbers caused many changes of training station.

The 1939 emergency put many early airwomen in charge of others with great responsibilities and little or no guidance or training. There was also some confusion on rank names, but by 1941 these had all been consolidated, modelled mainly on the RAF. By 1940 urgent training began for administrative non-commissioned officers (corporals and some sergeants) who had dealt almost exclusively with airwomen in their care. Special cases such as balloon operators

Badges of rank (1 being the highest). Badges were the same for RAF and WAAF, but many WAAF rank names differed from RAF.

and medical services trained elsewhere. Courses changed, adding senior NCO training (sergeants, flight sergeants and lastly warrant officers), and finally ended in 1946. It took a long time for women to become sufficiently experienced to be considered worthy of senior status.

Most pre-war officers started the Second World War as WAAF G (general) administrative officers, nicknamed *Queen Bees*. Woefully inexperienced, their quality and training was patchy and their responsibilities were vague. Later, officers were appointed on the spot by selection boards from the airwomen presented to them. In August 1942 an Officer Cadet Training Unit (OCTU) opened, in which suitable ex-airwomen had to pass an eight-week course *before* they were commissioned. Numbers fluctuated and OCTU members moved several times. Specialists such as code and cypher officers had their own courses.

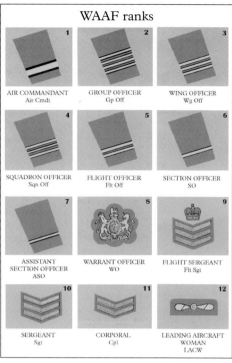

WAAF ranks

1 AIR COMMANDANT Air Cmdt	2 GROUP OFFICER Gp Off	3 WING OFFICER Wg Off
4 SQUADRON OFFICER Sqn Off	5 FLIGHT OFFICER Flt Off	6 SECTION OFFICER SO
7 ASSISTANT SECTION OFFICER ASO	8 WARRANT OFFICER WO	9 FLIGHT SERGEANT Flt Sgt
10 SERGEANT Sgt	11 CORPORAL Cpl	12 LEADING AIRCRAFT WOMAN LACW

The WAAF Commandant in Chief was the Queen, and in 1940 the Duchess of Gloucester began her affectionate connection with the WAAF, rising to Air Chief Commandant in 1943.

The Good Conduct Stripe on the lower left arm is awarded for three years of good conduct (or, according to an RAF saying, 'three years of undetected crime'!).

The first WAAF officers' course at Bulstrode Park, Gerrards Cross, Buckinghamshire, in spring 1941. The text that accompanies this newspaper photograph reads: 'Blossoming out into officers are these WAAFs training among the Daffs, somewhere in the home counties. For two weeks in a country mansion they undergo a course to fit them to command. Great attention is paid to physical training, and here a man takes charge of them in a secluded corner of the College for Commissions.'

The second WAAF director, Air Chief Commandant Lady Ruth Mary Eldridge Welsh DBE (1943–6) (left), with the Duchess of Gloucester (right), at an exhibition.

Pay and promotion

The fortnightly wage for airwomen was two-thirds of that of the RAF – itself not high. 'Never had so many waited so long for so little', they grumbled. Uniform, accommodation, food, medical care and dental care were free, and at the war's end airwomen were given a gratuity that amounted to two-thirds of that given to the RAF.

Basic training was usually followed by trade training, in mixed classes and under high pressure. From the lowest rank of Aircraftwoman 2nd Class (with no distinguishing badges), WAAF had hopes of promotion, along with pay increases, once they were fully trained and experienced. Many, however, rejected commissions to become officers, preferring to remain with their friends in the ranks.

DAILY RATES OF PAY OF AIRWOMEN OF THE WOMEN'S AUXILIARY AIR FORCE.

Rank.	Group II.	Group III.	Group IV.	Group V.
	s. d.	s. d.	s. d.	s. d.
Aircraftwoman 2nd Class	2 4	2 0	2 2	1 4†
Aircraftwoman 1st Class	2 10	2 6	2 8	2 4
Corporal (earlier, Assistant Section Leader) ..	4 4	3 4	3 8	3 0
Sergeant (earlier, Section Leader)	5 8	4 4	4 8	4 0
Senior Sergeant (earlier, Senior Section Leader, later, Flight Sergeant)	6 8	5 4	5 8	5 2
*Under Officer		Rates not	yet fixed.	

* Establishment not yet agreed.
† Cooks who are accepted as fully qualified will be entitled on entry to pay at the rate of 2s. a day. Other entrants in this trade will receive 1s. 4d. a day on entry, rising to 1s. 8d., and subsequently 2s. a day when fully qualified.

DAILY RATES OF PAY OF AIRWOMEN OF THE WOMEN'S AUXILIARY AIR FORCE.

Rank	Group I	Group II	Group III	Group IV	Group V *	Group M †
	s. d.	s. d.	s. d.	s. d.	s. d.	s. d.
Aircraftwoman, 2nd Class	3 2	3 0	2 8	2 10	2 0	2 0
Over 6 months ..	—	—	—	—	2 4	2 4
Over 1 year	—	—	—	—	2 8	2 8
Over 2 years	—	—	—	—		2 10
Aircraftwoman, 1st Class	3 8	3 6	3 2	3 4	3 0	3 2
Leading Aircraftwoman	4 4	4 0	3 6	3 8	3 4	3 6
Over 3 years	4 8	4 4	3 8	4 0	3 6	3 10
Corporal	5 8	5 0	4 0	4 4	3 10	4 2
Over 3 years	—	—	—	—		4 8
Over 4 years	6 0	5 4	4 4	4 4	4 0	
Sergeant	7 0	6 4	5 0	5 4	4 8	5 4
Over 3 years	—	—	—	—		6 0
Over 4 years	7 4	6 8	5 4	5 8	5 0	
Flight Sergeant	8 4	7 4	6 0	6 4	5 10	7 0
Over 3 years	—	—	—	—		7 8
Over 4 years	8 8	7 8	6 4	6 8	6 0	
Warrant Officer	10 0	9 0	8 4	8 4	8 4	9 8
Over 5 years	11 8	10 8	9 8	10 0	9 8	

From 1st July, 1946, the above rates will be increased by 8d. a day. Airwomen already serving on that date will receive 8d. a day above their existing rates of pay.

* Under certain conditions additional pay is issuable to airwomen employed as interpreters, crews of aircraft, schoolmistresses, trumpeters, W.A.A.F. police, physical training instructors and M.T. drivers.

† A qualified nursing orderly or dental clerk orderly may receive the over-one-years'-service rate for an aircraftwoman 2nd class in Group M on entry or remustering to the trade of nursing orderly or dental clerk orderly.

Compare the daily rates of pay towards the beginning of the Second World War (October 1940, above) with those after the war had ended (July 1946, left). During the war a small house cost around £200–£500, a large loaf of bread 4¹⁄₂d, and a cup of tea and a bun at the NAAFI 2d. (Air Ministry Pamphlet 103, second and eighth editions)

Trades

Domestic trades

The Domestic Group, including orderlies and batwomen, was the largest and among the hardest worked of all trades. In around 1940 a few WAAF catering officers appeared, some attached to hospitals. In 1943 a total of 23,034 WAAF members formed about 54 per cent of all cooks, soon rising to 61 per cent. In order to pass her trade tests as an 'ACW2', a cook preparing food for hundreds had to learn how to judge quantities, cut and assess different joints of meat, practise field cookery and cater for different diets – along with many other skills. On both day and night shifts, cooks had to accommodate a variety of needs: those of weary but hungry aircrew returning at dawn and wanting bacon and eggs before bed, or those of watch-keepers in busy operations rooms needing cocoa and meals during long nights. A WAAF food ration was four-fifths that of her male counterpart in the RAF, but this became easier when mixed messing (dining) began.

Technical trades

By the 1940s, boys and girls between the ages of about five and eleven normally had a good primary education, particularly in the 'three Rs'. Girls may not have been encouraged to the same extent as boys in mathematics, but they were able to gain notable reading and writing skills. *Further* education for girls rarely included the scientific or technical subjects usually offered to boys. Consequently, when manpower shortages forced the RAF to introduce technical trades for WAAF, it started by breaking them down into simple components and was

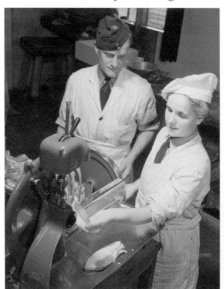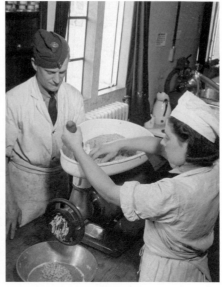

A WAAF recruit under training to be a cook and butcher, 1940.

11

An airwoman training in a mixed class on battery charging.

surprised to find how quickly the girls picked them up. In late 1940, in order to release more men for flying duties, an Air Ministry Committee agreed that 'no work should be done by a man if a woman could do it or be trained to do it'. Thus by 1941 such experimental trades as sparking-plug tester, charging-board operator and a simpler instrument repairer came into being.

Once the competence of airwomen was realised, a wider range of technical trades opened up to them, starting with the more difficult *mechanic* level, including mechanical transport (MT), radar and flight mechanic, and followed later by the more advanced *fitter* trades for the most highly skilled. In some of the earlier trades women substituted for men in a ratio of three

TWO SIX W

W.A.A.F. FITTERS

Invite you to

1st Entry Passing-Out Dance

in

BURNETT GYM.

on **Monday, 24th May, 1943**

Irene Stocks B381

An invitation to a passing-out dance.

Leading Aircraftwoman Joyce Wallace, a flight mechanic, taking a break and sitting on the wing of a Spitfire during a routine check at Dunsfold airfield, Surrey. She had remustered after being a balloon operator and now worked on Typhoons, Tempests and later Meteors.

A telephonist at work at the telephone console in the operations room of RAF Barkway, Hertfordshire, 1944-5.

to one but, with the later male deficit, the ratio sometimes reached one to one. Nineteen trades were entirely in the hands of WAAF, such as the WAAF police, dental hygienists and wireless telegraphy slip readers, while women were barred from certain RAF trades such as aircrew.

Communications and intelligence work

The Signals Branch, which included radar, employed nearly 32,000 WAAF in September 1944. It handled the fast communication of messages by telephone or teleprinter in 'clear' (words), mainly at home, and in morse, mainly from home to abroad, the more secret being in code. For this purpose British embassies abroad were allocated code and cypher officers, most of whom were from the WAAF, with a total of 1231 officers employed in mid 1943. Prime Minister Churchill's own War Cabinet Cypher Office in London was run by the WAAF, and some of these officers travelled with him to his big conferences abroad, handling his secret signals traffic, assisted from 1943 by a few airwomen.

Sir Robert Watson-Watt had developed the idea of radar so successfully that by early 1939 there were already twenty radar stations in an unbroken chain along the south and east coasts of Britain, and these spread from 1940 along the west coast. The RAF depended on these stations for early warning so that it could effectively direct its aircraft for defence and attack. Originally known as Radio Direction-Finding (RDF), it was not until 1942 that this system was christened 'radar' (radio detection and ranging) by the American navy. Sir Robert believed that women's 'anti-hamfistedness' would make them ideal operators and so they were among the earliest trade recruits of the wartime WAAF, though for secrecy, like plotters, they were known as Special Duties Clerks (clks sd).

Radar pylons at Danby Beacon, North Yorkshire.

13

An early interception room of Ground Control Interception (GCI) by radar direction. The picture shows work in the 'Happidrome', guiding planes into position for attack on enemy raiders.

The Telecommunications Research Establishment, Malvern, Worcestershire, produced many radar systems such as the navigation aid GEE for aeroplanes and developed H_2S ground-mapping radar and OBOE for the bombing accuracy needed by such as pathfinders. It was chiefly WAAF personnel who operated the radar systems, in flimsy huts or concrete structures underground, straining their eyes on the lines and blips of their television-like screens and passing their information to filter rooms and tellers who forwarded it to operations rooms. Here, with rakes like those used by croupiers, plotters, again usually WAAF, marked the position of all aircraft on huge plotting tables, sometimes pressing headphones to their ears to keep out the din of exploding bombs. By July 1943 there were 7395 Special Duties Clerks, who were overworked but appreciated – as they had been in the 1940 Battle of Britain, in which, against all expectation, they had worked on, unfazed.

Another use of radio was in the Y Listening Service, where Jean Conan Doyle, a future WRAF director, worked. Here, with headphones clamped to their ears and twiddling dials on their sets, many WAAF operatives, fluent in languages, logged every word, number or message heard on the air waves. These intercepts added to the volume of collected information passed by dispatch riders to Bletchley Park (Station X) in Buckinghamshire. Special sections watched for messages from Special Operations Executive (SOE) agents. As part of Radar Counter Measures (RCM), some German-speaking WAAF took part in operation *Corona*, feeding false information and coordinates to mislead German pilots, who, thinking they came from their own ground station, sometimes landed by mistake in England.

In the 1930s Polish code-breakers produced a copy of the Enigma machine used by the German armed forces to send secret messages. The Polish replica was

passed to the French and English in the summer of 1939. Despite having different daily settings, the machine helped the unconventional and brilliant staff at Bletchley Park – which employed about 10,000 people, civilian and service, including some WAAF – in their slow process of breaking and reading

On watch in a signals cabin, 1945.

14

Left: *The Bombe, developed by Alan Turing at Bletchley Park, Buckinghamshire, to break Enigma codes.*

Right: *The Enigma cypher machine used by the German army and air force, and the code-breakers at Bletchley Park.*

in secret the constantly changing enemy codes and ciphers. Later inventions, such as the electro-mechanical Bombes and the even more sophisticated Colossus, also helped with the code-breaking. Combined with other sources, this information, called 'Ultra' (and, in the RAF, 'Fred'), saved many lives and probably shortened the war by two years. Churchill called the code-breakers 'the geese that laid the golden eggs but never cackled'. Bletchley Park closed in 1946, still shrouded in secrecy.

Information was also collected by photographers and air interpreters. WAAF station photographers normally had civil experience. By 1943, numbering 383, their work was usually mundane, but they occasionally serviced aircraft cameras. In 1941, RAF Medmenham, Buckinghamshire, had become the centre of photographic air interpretation, eventually employing 1715 people, of whom over 1270 were RAF and 130 WAAF; the latter included Sarah Churchill and Constance Babington-Smith. Working on black and white reconnaissance photographs, interpreters strove to elicit useful intelligence from the spy-in-the-sky cameras. Maps were also created from a

Constance Babington-Smith, here bent over to study closely a photographic detail. It was her identification from an aerial photograph of a V1 flying bomb on its launch ramp at Peenemunde in November 1943 that enabled the RAF, by destroying the sites in Operation Crossbow, to delay their attack until late 1944.

A balloon crew on Site 5 at Osmaston Park, Derbyshire, in late 1942 with their winch, used to raise and lower their balloon.

complicated multi-stereographic 'Wild' machine in Z Section, backed by highly skilled modellers of important land masses and targets. All worked closely with Bletchley Park.

Barrage-balloon girls

A vast barrage of silver balloons was already guarding London when the Second World War began. WAAF were not considered strong enough to control the huge thrashing bags of gas in high winds, many of which were armed to explode if touched by an enemy raider. Nevertheless, in May 1941, 257 'Young Amazons' were cautiously introduced. By 1943, 1029 balloon sites were run by all-women crews, forming 47 per cent of Balloon Command personnel. Crews, normally comprising twelve airwomen and two non-commissioned officers, had extra rations and accommodation, and loved their work. However, this WAAF trade was gradually phased out from 1944 because of injuries and overseas RAF commitments.

Medical trades

Nursing sisters of the Princess Mary's RAF Nursing Service (PMRAFNS) were joined on 1st September 1939 by WAAF medical orderlies, recruited to assist them, followed by WAAF dental surgery attendants, but a separate medical trade group did not emerge until August 1940. WAAF nursing orderlies appeared in hospitals with a number of ancillary trades in the following year, many bringing

16

civilian experience with them. By June 1943, 214 WAAF air-ambulance orderlies had been trained and used on flights in Britain, but later many were flown to Europe to bring back wounded servicemen from around the battle sites, such speedy evacuation saving many lives. There were also a few female medical officers (doctors), categorised not as WAAF but RAF.

Other trades

There were many other types of work done by WAAF airwomen and officers. Equippers could deal with anything from aircraft parts to clothing. Mechanical-transport drivers operated vehicles ranging from tractors for bombing-up aircraft to 3 ton lorries. Electricians undertook concentrated three-year courses in a mere nine months. On the skilled fingers of parachute packers rested the lives of aircrew, as they did on the

A WAAF nursing orderly on a Dakota air ambulance in 1944, tending stretcher cases evacuated from France.

Two WAAF, who joined the Air Transport Auxiliary, in their flying suits at Barton-in-the-Clay, Bedfordshire, 1945.

accurate work of meteorologists. Although WAAF did not fly (except by luck, accident, or to carry out air checks), the Air Transport Auxiliary (ATA) shortages caused the RAF to allow thirty WAAF to join – out of 1400 volunteers. Assistant armourers learned weaponry, and for emergencies, though unofficial, WAAF weapons training was sometimes given.

Airwomen's trades, 1946. (Air Ministry Pamphlet 103, eighth edition)

Group I	Group II	Group III	Group IV	Group V	Group M
Draughtswoman (cartographical). Electrician I. Fitter II (air frame). Fitter II (engine) High-speed telegraphist. Instrument repairer I. Model maker. Radar mechanic. Wireless mechanic. Wireless operator mechanic.	Acetylene welder. Aircraft finisher. Armourer (guns). Balloon operator. Carpenter. Cook. Electrician, grade II. Flight mechanic (air frame). Flight mechanic (engine). Interpreter (technical). Instrument repairer, grade II. Meteorologist. M.T. mechanic. Photographer. Radar operator. Safety equipment worker. Wireless operator. W.T. (slip reader operator).	Cook. Fabric worker, aero. Fabric worker, balloon. Hairdresser. Radio assistant. Safety equipment assistant. Shoe repairer. Tailor. Telephonist.	Administrative. Air movements assistant. Clerk, equipment accounting. Clerk, general duties. Clerk, general duties (cypher). Clerk (movement control). Clerk, pay accounting. Clerk, personnel selection. Clerk (provisioning). Clerk (signals). Clerk (special duties). Clerk, special duties (watchkeeper). Equipment assistant. Interpreter. *Radar operator. R.T. operator. Teleprinter operator. Tracer.	Aircrafthand general duties. Armament assistant. Balloon parachute hand. Batwoman. Bomb plotter. Cine projectionist. Drogue packer and repairer. M.T. driver. Maintenance assistant. Mess steward. Orderly. Physical training instructor. Waitress. W.A.A.F. police.	Chiropodist. Dental clerk orderly. Dental hygienist. Dispenser. Laboratory assistant. Masseuse. Nursing orderly. Operating room assistant. Optician orderly. Radiographer.

* Group II after 6 months' efficient service.

18

Officer Branches	Operations 'B'
Accountant	Operations 'C'
Administrative	Orthoptist
Catering	Personnel Selection
Code and Cypher	Photographic Interpretation
Equipment	Provost
Filter	Signals 'G'
Intelligence	Signals, Special Radar
Interception Controller	Signals, Supervisory Radar
Medical and Psychological Assistant	WAAF G (WAAF only)
Meteorological	Dentist (RAF Branch)
Motor Transport	Doctor (RAF Branch)
Movements Liaison	

WAAF officer branches, 1946. (AP3234)

Unusual WAAF involvements

During the Second World War, the WAAF became involved in a wide variety of unusual jobs other than code-breaking and Special Operations Executive work. Many were highly secret and, having signed the Official Secrets Acts, no WAAF would speak of them until many years later. The following is a small selection: one driver waited to pick up captured German parachutists from abortive drops on the South Downs; another caught a German spy on her secret wireless frequency; one X-rayed the joints of PLUTO – the rubber pipe used to take petrol to D-Day France from England; others helped in experiments on FIDO (Fog Intensification Dispersal Operations), Window (radar jamming by jettisoning strips of silver foil) and the first use of penicillin on the RAF wounded.

An eyewitness sketch, by the WAAF driver on duty at the time, of the RAF Swingate Guard Room, Dover, on the night of 11–12th July 1940, when German parachutists landed on the Downs.

19

Everyday life

Accommodation and living conditions

When war began, stations often boarded out their WAAF – sometimes during training (WAAF were not favourites with landladies!). Occasionally a WAAF Hostel would be a requisitioned house or hall, often more comfortable than the traditional living quarters on camp. Training completed, the girls were posted to their normal stations, where soon they were accommodated in huts – either wooden ones with Tarmac roofs or corrugated steel ones in the shape of a half-moon; rare were the WAAF who lived in brick-built barracks. Airwomen's

sleeping and dining (mess) huts were fenced off (with their own guardroom) from the rest of the camp and the airmen, who usually far outnumbered them.

Living and working conditions on camp were usually cold and spartan, but the girls endured them, knowing the hardships of their fellow airmen. In huts, hot water and heat depended on one temperamental pot-bellied black stove, with fuel tightly rationed. One window was left open all night, whatever the weather – icicles sometimes formed from the ceiling. Rats and mice were common room-mates. Bathrooms and toilets (ablutions) were often in distant huts; greatcoat-clad girls had to dash across the fields morning and night! Washing and showering was communal, bath water restricted to a 4 inch (10 cm) line painted on the bath. 'Cleanliness may be next to godliness,' commented one girl, 'but it sure

Three types of accommodation: (top) requisitioned Gatcombe Park, Gloucestershire, 1943; (centre) a hut – still in use; (bottom) a Nissen hut at Allerton Park, near Knaresborough, North Yorkshire, 1943.

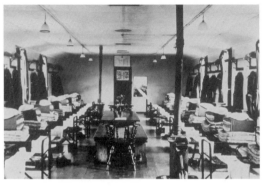

A typical hut interior. Note the stove, bed packs and polished linoleum.

Below: *WAAF kit, laid out for inspection, 1944.*

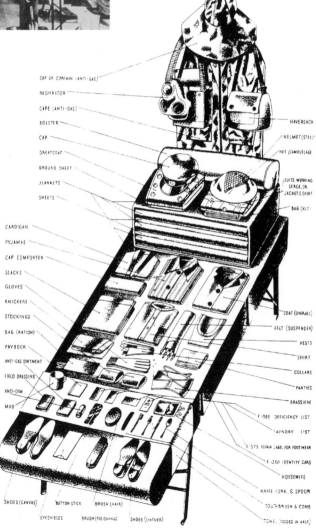

CAP OR CURTAIN (ANTI-GAS)
RESPIRATOR
CAPE (ANTI-GAS)
BOLSTER
CAP
GREATCOAT
GROUND SHEET
BLANKETS
SHEETS
CARDIGAN
PYJAMAS
CAP COMFORTER
SLACKS
GLOVES
KNICKERS
STOCKINGS
BAG (RATION)
PAYBOOK
ANTI-GAS OINTMENT
FIELD DRESSINGS
ANTI-DIM
MUG

HAVERSACK
HELMET (STEEL)
NET (CAMOUFLAGE)
SUITS, WORKING SERGE, OR JACKET & SKIRT
BAG (KIT)
COAT (OVERALL)
BELT (SUSPENDER)
VESTS
SHIRT
COLLARS
PANTIES
BRASSIERE
F 1583 DEFICIENCY LIST
LAUNDRY LIST
F 575 REPAIR LABEL FOR FOOTWEAR
F 1250 IDENTITY CARD
HOUSEWIFE
KNIFE, FORK, & SPOON
TOOTHBRUSH & COMB
TOWEL, FOLDED IN HALF)

SHOES (CANVAS)   BUTTON STICK   BRUSH (HAIR)
EYESHIELDS   BRUSH (POLISHING)   SHOES (LEATHER)

has its problems in winter.'

At first uniforms were often insufficient and ill-fitting, despite the efforts of over-worked WAAF tailoresses. Shoes (beetle-crushers), black, flat and bulled nightly to a high gloss, were painfully broken in. Underwear, dating from the First World War, frequently caused gales of laughter when it was paraded at night in the huts, but girls from poor homes revelled in having so many clothes, and uniform was a great leveller. Steel helmets were useful for showers, and anti-gas capes and Lord Nuffield's gift of sanitary towels found many uses. Everything had to be labelled, including personal mugs and cutlery (irons). All items had to be laid out in a prescribed pattern for monthly kit inspection, with heavy

21

DEFICIENT ITEMS. (All entries are to be made in ink).				
Section	Reference No.	ITEM	Quantity	Issued on I.V. No.
22c	472	haversacks waaf	1	

Unused lines are to be struck through by the Issuing Officer.

The kit deficiency form. Items listed incurred a heavy fine.

fines for any items found to be missing.

Once-weekly domestic nights, suffered by the WAAF but not the RAF, confined girls to their huts for special cleaning sessions and to bring clothes up to standard. Grey cotton stockings, for example, had to be darned constantly, as they could rarely be exchanged at monthly clothing parades. Beds had to be changed weekly and free laundry collected, but some girls preferred to have their collars starched by Chinese laundries. Unappreciated by most WAAF, these domestic nights could nevertheless create a family spirit. When all was finished, girls would sit around their stove chatting, doing hair, writing letters, swapping 'lost' items, helping one another with various chores, and drinking cocoa. Lights were out around 10.30.

Prize-winning WAAF wearing service summer (lightweight, silky and lilac) knickers, nicknamed 'twilights', 1945–6.

The WAAF contingent passing the saluting base in the Market Place, Derby, during the opening of 'Salute the Soldier' Week, 3rd May 1944.

Parades

WAAF did not do as much marching as the public believed. Of course there were weekly commanding officer parades and special ones for events such as recruiting, Wings for Victory, Battle of Britain, royal occasions, investitures and VIP visitors, and there were annual Air Officer Commanding (AOC) parades. WAAF usually marched with the RAF, but they were separated into flights, and the two groups vied with each other for smartness.

When mishaps occurred it set the girls giggling. Parades also brought together those who often worked in far-flung areas of large camps and gave them all fresh air and exercise. In fine weather and with a good band – occasionally WAAF – they came to enjoy parading, but shift work and priority trades frequently prevented some from taking part.

Discipline

Normally WAAF were well behaved, but sometimes they had to be tried in their WAAF officer's Orderly Room for minor misdemeanours such as turning up late for something. Most punishments involved fines, extra duties (fatigues) or CB ('confined to barracks'). More serious charges such as theft or absence without leave took offenders before the commanding officer or even the very rare court martial. One such trial was for losing a barrage balloon, for which the girl got off!

Criticisms levelled at all three women's services resulted in the Markham report, which scotched accusations of loose morality and found the incidence of venereal disease and illegitimate births low in comparison with that among civilians. The Air Ministry, conscious of its duty in the place of parents, took great care of its WAAF.

Sports and leisure

Sport was encouraged on camp. Tennis, netball and hockey were usually to be found, but most girls were not keen on sport, which in any case, they saw, tended to be reserved only for the best players. Apart from these infrequent games, work took up most sports afternoons, though a few stations held a (mixed) Annual

A cup being presented to the winners of the inter-station netball tournament, 1945.

Below: *A physical-training display for Queen Mary at Badminton House, Gloucestershire, 1943.*

Sports Day, when duties allowed. Physical training was avoided if possible – but the RAF wanted to keep the WAAF fit!

When off duty, girls loved exploring the local area, frequently in groups and on bicycles. Although few airwomen had their own transport, bicycles were popular, often loaned out from a station pool. When bicycles were not available it was necessary for the girls to thumb a lift or to use one of the four free train warrants allocated each year. The odd person might have a horse or a car, but petrol was almost unobtainable. Postings to other camps (rating free travel warrants) ranged from no moves to many – one WAAF counted fifteen in five years!

The Navy, Army and Air Force Institute (NAAFI) was the main centre for socialising and relaxation, and it was here that girls could buy snacks, drinks and cigarettes. Some camps ran competitions, exhibitions and clubs for crafts and suchlike. The girls, far outnumbered by RAF, revelled in the regularly held station dances and parties in the NAAFI, often with their own RAF band, which

Below: *A corner of the NAAFI at RAF Wythall, Worcestershire.*

Above: *Cover, while changing on the beach for a swim – a new use for a gas cape, Withernsea, East Yorkshire, 1944. Note the anti-tank defences.*

)·11·4-1
— 14·11· 41·

PROGRAMME

OF ATTRACTIONS FOR

NOVEMBER, 1941

FOUR CHANGES OF PROGRAMME WEEKLY

TIMES OF SHOWING.

Weekdays : Continuous performance from 6.15 p.m.
Last complete performance commences 8.15 p.m. approx.
Sundays : 2.0, 5.30 and 7.30 p.m.

Prices of
Admission **6d., 9d. and 1/-**

The Cinema is fully equipped with Modern Projectors
Sound Apparatus, and Comfortable Theatre Seats.

A THOROUGHLY ENTERTAINING SHOW
AND IT COSTS YOU SO LITTLE

All Programmes are subject to alteration at the discretion
of the Management

A cinema programme at Bridgnorth, Shropshire, November 1941.

UP-TO-DATE BRITISH MOVIETONE NEWS EVERYDAY

DATE	FEATURE FILM	STARS
Mon & Tues Nov. 3rd & 4th	TWO FOR DANGER	Barry K. Barnes, Greta Gynt, Cecil Parker
Wed & Thurs Nov. 5th & 6th	MY LITTLE CHICKADEE	Mae West, W. C. Fields, Joseph Callela
Fri & Sat Nov. 7th & 8th	We're in The Army Now	Jane Withers, Ritz Bros., Lynn Bari
Mon & Tues Nov. 10th & 11th	Broadway Melody of 1940	Fred Astaire, Eleanor Powell, George Murphy
Wed & Thurs Nov. 12th & 13th	YEARS WITHOUT DAYS	John Garfield, Ann Sheridan
Fri & Sat Nov. 14th & 15th	BARRICADE	Alice Faye, Warner Baxter, Charles Winninger
Mon & Tues Nov. 17th & 18th	FORTY LITTLE MOTHERS	Eddie Cantor, Judith Anderson, Baby Quantanilla
Wed & Thurs Nov. 19th & 20th	VIRGINIA CITY	Errol Flynn, Marian Hopkins, Randolph Scott
Fri & Sat Nov. 21st & 22nd	Cisco Kid and The Lady	Cesar Romero, Marjorie Weaver, Chris-Pin Martin
Mon & Tues Nov. 24th & 25th	CHOSE YOUR PARTNER	Lana Turner, Joan Blondell, George Murphy
Wed & Thurs Nov. 26th & 27th	BOY MEETS GIRL	James Cagney, Pat O'Brien, Marie Wilson
Fri & Sat Nov. 28th & 29th	Everything Happens at Night	Sonja Henie, Ray Milland, Robert Cummings
	SUNDAYS	
Nov. 2nd	Thirteen Men and A Gun	Arthur Wontner, H. Marion-Crawford
Nov. 9th	Pack Up Your Troubles	Wally Patch, Muriel George, Ernest Butcher
Nov. 16th	WOLF'S CLOTHING	Gordon Harker, Claude Hulbert, Lilli Palmer
Nov. 23rd	JAILBIRDS	Albert Burdon, Shaun Glenville, Charles Farrell, Charles Hawtrey
Nov. 30th	SCARFACE	Paul Muni, George Raft, Boris Karloff

SUPPORT YOUR OWN CINEMA

sometimes lent its efforts to church services. These were normally popular – unlike church parades, which took up an otherwise free morning.

Stations, large and small, usually had a cinema with a constantly changing programme. Local pubs were also popular. The Entertainments National Service Association (ENSA), where stars and others gave their skills free, did its best to put on occasional live shows and concerts, particularly for remote small stations or for camps abroad. Station variety shows and drama groups flourished, nurturing some future famous talents. In London and other towns, theatres occasionally offered free seats to service folk, and big dance-halls were ever attractive to dance-mad girls – though here *men* were in short supply! Certain clubs also gave cheap accommodation to the cash-strapped service personnel, and sometimes WAAF were guests in benevolent civilian homes.

The high point of the year was Christmas, full of parties, official and

WAAF of the West Malling (Kent) concert party, May 1945.

25

The Christmas menu and programme at RAF Watton, Norfolk, 1942 – with drink stains.

unofficial. Christmas dinner was special: officers and NCOs came to serve both men and girls with food, carefully hoarded for months by the cooks. Holly, paper chains and lanterns decorated all available space.

Around this time, WAAF and RAF entertained local children and orphans, giving out gifts and wonderful food, and WAAF helped their favourite charities. They visited the sick in hospitals and homes, and in London a few walked with blinded St Dunstan aircrew.

All in all, WAAF girls were a self-sufficient bunch. They often found much to laugh at and unorthodox ways around problems, besides being good at bending the rules to their advantage.

A Christmas party given by WAAF for children in the NAAFI at RAF Heslington, North Yorkshire.

26

Bravery awards

WAAF showed great bravery in many dangerous situations, often unremarked, 'because it was the only thing to do!'. Among the lower awards recognising this were 2497 **Mentions in Despatches (MIDs)** and many **Commendations**. Higher awards included ninety-seven **Members of the Order of the British Empire (MBEs)** and ninety-three **British Empire Medals (BEMs)** – three for *special gallantry*. Leading Aircraftwoman Kathleen McKinlay, a driver, took her ambulance through heavy shelling at Dover. Corporal Alice Holden, a telephonist, pulled a pilot from an exploding Wellington bomber. Leading Aircraftwoman Lilian Ellis kept her balloon flying and organised first aid for four wounded airwomen when a bomb went off, killing three. An ordinary BEM went to Leading Aircraftwoman Ivy Cross, a driver, who twelve times in one year was the first on the scene to help aircrew from crashed bombers.

All six **Military Medals (MMs)** of the Second World War went to WAAF for bravery in air raids. Realising the importance of the information needing to be passed on,

Right: *Corporal Alice Holden, special gallantry BEM.*

Left: *Leading Aircraftwoman Ivy Cross, BEM.*

The British Empire Medal.

27

telephonists Corporal Henderson and Sergeant Turner refused to leave their burning building until nearly too late. Sergeant Mary Youle encouraged her telephonists to continue working, despite the destruction of part of their exchange. When a bomb killed and injured many sheltering in the dugout with her, Corporal Josephine Robins gave first aid and helped in its evacuation. Sergeant Joan Mortimer was injured while placing red flags around unexploded bombs to warn incoming planes. Acting Corporal Avis Hearn, a lone radar operator, steadily passed on the course of enemy bombers, with bombs and debris falling almost on her head.

About an hour after midnight in May 1940, Corporal Daphne Pearson, a sick-quarter attendant at RAF Detling in Kent, heard an incoming aeroplane crash nearby. Immediately she ran to the field and helped release the pilot from the burning wreckage. As she unclipped his harness he muttered that he had bombs on board, ready to go off. She dragged him about 30 yards (27 metres) away just before the petrol tanks and a bomb exploded, when she threw herself on top of him and put her helmet over his head to protect him. Then she helped move him to the ambulance after more bombs went off. Returning afterwards she could not rescue the last man, but her bravery had saved the pilot's life. For this selfless act Corporal Daphne Pearson received the **Empire Gallantry Medal (EGM)**, later changed to the George Cross.

Right: Corporal Daphne Pearson was awarded the Empire Gallantry Medal, later exchanged for the George Cross.

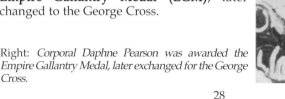

Far left: *Muriel Byck, MID, was a wireless operator for four months. She died in France of meningitis.*

Left: *Diana Rowden, MID, was a courier for one month. She died by lethal injection at Natzweiler Concentration Camp. Her MBE was withdrawn when the award was found to have post-dated her death.*

In July 1940, Winston Churchill set up a small secret organisation in Britain that was dedicated to helping the resistance to the enemy. It was named the **Special Operations Executive (SOE)**. It employed several thousand service and civilian men and women in Britain and sent some hastily trained agents into enemy-occupied countries, not as spies but to help the resistance with sabotage. **'F' Section** sent to France about four hundred agents, around fifty being women, thirty-six of them British. Agents, usually in groups of three – organiser, courier and wireless operator – worked with the resistance and maquis in an allocated area, their days so fraught with danger that many lost their lives to the German Gestapo. All were volunteers and showed extraordinary courage. Few who died received higher British awards.

The small numbers of SOE agents with the resistance in France were worth ten to fifteen divisions of regular troops and probably shortened the war by nine months. Some WAAF with French backgrounds were transferred to SOE and fifteen became agents, who, to avoid the official WAAF embargo on using lethal

Right: *Yvonne Cormeau, MBE, was a wireless operator who sent over four hundred perfect transmissions in thirteen months. She survived.*

Far right: *Pearl Witherington, MBE, was a courier and then a most successful organiser, with around ten thousand maquis under her control. She survived, having served in France for fifteen months.*

Far left: *Noor-un-Nisa Inayat Khan, GC.*

Left: *The George Cross.*

weapons, trained in the First Aid Nursing Yeomanry (FANYs). They were sent to France, eight in the most vulnerable trade of wireless operator (w/op). Twelve, being airwomen, were made honorary officers in the hope that if captured they would be better treated. They were not! Six died; ten received MBEs. Apart from those pictured were: Yvonne Baseden, w/op, survived Ravensbruck; Yolande Beekman, w/op, shot at Dachau; Sonya Butt, courier, survived; Mary Herbert, courier, survived; Phyllis Latour, w/op, survived; Cécile Lefort, courier, died at Ravensbruck; Patricia O'Sullivan, w/op, survived; Lilian Rolfe, w/op, shot at Ravensbruck; Anne-Marie Walters, courier, survived.

A recipient of the **George Cross (GC)**, Princess Noor-un-Nisa Inayat Khan, daughter of an Indian Sufi leader, was brought up in Paris. In 1940, fleeing the Germans, she joined the WAAF and became a wireless operator. On transferring to SOE she was sent as the first female wireless operator to Paris in 1943, despite the SOE's warning that the chances of a wireless operator surviving for more than about six weeks were slim. Shortly after her arrival the group in which she was working was broken up by the Gestapo. Knowing she was the last radio link with London, she refused to return to safety. In October she was betrayed, taken to the Gestapo headquarters and interrogated, but she would not implicate her helpers.

She almost escaped twice, ending up chained in a solitary-confinement cell at Pforzheim Prison. On 12th September 1944 at Dachau Concentration Camp, with three other SOE women, holding hands in pairs and kneeling, she was shot. Her last word was 'Liberté!'

The incredible exploits of Christine Granville (Countess Kristina Gizycka), in assisting resistance and escape lines in the Middle East and Europe to help free her beloved Poland, led her to be called the 'Polish Pimpernel' and to be suspected by all sides as a spy, even though she was loosely connected with British Intelligence and, latterly, the SOE. With her energy, intelligence, flair for languages and magnetic

Christine Granville, GM.

30

charm, she was virtually a free agent. As an SOE courier in 1944, she escaped from a massed German attack on her Vercors headquarters. Later she rescued her organiser by a trick, and several times with great audacity turned around the loyalties of non-German troops. For her remarkable work Christine Granville was awarded the **George Medal (GM)**.

The Special Intelligence Service (**SIS**) worked for the British Foreign Office, or MI6. Because it expected the greater share of supplies and aircraft, it did not agree with the independent SOE. The loud bangs caused by SOE sabotage were anathema to the SIS, endangering its agents' inconspicuous presence. The SIS sent intelligence-gathering spies, of whom Sibyl Sturrock was one, all over the world.

From a WAAF Sergeant wireless operator, she was seconded to the SIS in 1944 and parachuted into the tangled political situation of Yugoslavia, where she had

once lived. Here the Allies gradually sided with the communist Tito's partisans as their resistance to the Germans was more effective. In the winter snow, on foot and horseback, Sibyl Sturrock accompanied the partisans until they joined with the Russian Red Army and finally liberated Zagreb. Her bravery earned her an MBE.

Sibyl Sturrock, MBE.

The badge of a Member of the British Empire.

The WAAF abroad

The first WAAF to go abroad were the code and cypher officers who were sent to the British High Commission, New York, in 1940. They became part of the RAF Delegation in Washington in 1941 and, when the United States of America entered the Second World War, these officers' work and numbers increased and officers from five other branches arrived. As the North African offensive built up, a few WAAF officers were sent to Egypt and Palestine in 1941 among a sometimes hostile population, spitting and throwing stones. When the war moved, so did they (and other branches after 1943), to such places as the Bahamas, Bermuda, Newfoundland, Labrador, Algeria and the Far East, as well as to Europe after D-Day. In 1941 a few officers went to help with the Women's Division of the Royal Canadian Air Force, and they were joined in 1943 by some code and cypher officers. Nevertheless, despite the wide spread of WAAF around the world, the total numbers abroad never exceeded nine thousand.

The Middle East

Early attempts to enlist Palestinian women into the WAAF succeeded in attracting only eight hundred recruits. So, after the new director had checked everything carefully, the first draft of 250 volunteer British airwomen and their officers sailed to Egypt in 1944, mainly to carry out clerical, equipment and signals duties. After blacked-out Britain, the airwomen thought the lights of Alexandria 'just like fairyland'. Despite high temperatures, fleas, dysentery and sandstorms, the girls enjoyed Egypt (and, later, Palestine, Syria and Iraq). They worked hard, found discipline more relaxed than at home and holidayed in exotic locations never before possible for most of them. In 1945–6 they were allowed to exchange their warm blue uniforms of home for the much-resented khaki cotton drill. By late 1945, numbers of airwomen in the Middle East had risen to nearly 3500.

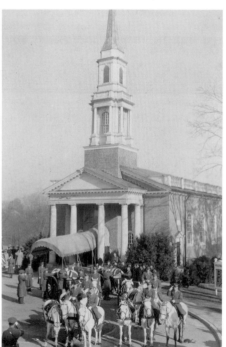

The funeral of Section Officer Monica Daventry and Section Officer Ruth Watson, WAAF code and cypher officers in Washington. They were killed in a car accident coming off duty in November 1943 and buried in Arlington National Cemetery, in the United States.

32

At Christmas 1945 a group of WAAF and RAF (some on camels) pay a visit to Giza, Egypt, to see the pyramids.

Below: *An aerial view of RAF station Ramleh, Palestine, 1945.*

India and Ceylon

Uniform problems and accommodation had been settled by the time the first airwomen and officers left for India to do many types of work. With the secrecy surrounding any overseas posting, none knew their destination until the ship docked at Bombay in November 1944. More airwomen followed, but at their highest, numbers never exceeded eight hundred. The work and climate were so enervating that two leave centres were set up at Conoor and Lower Topa in the hills. Later drafts of nearly five hundred went to Ceylon, where the damp heat proved trying despite the breezy bamboo huts in which the airwomen lived. In 1946, as part of the gradual withdrawal from India, the WAAF started to leave for Hong Kong and Singapore.

Algeria and the Mediterranean

Although WAAF cypher officers went to Algiers (and then Tunis) in 1943, airwomen did

A WAAF corporal checks the Christmas 1944 postal charges in India with the help of an airman interpreter.

33

not go there until the summer of 1945. The sunlight and the scent of orange trees charmed some, but others were depressed by the prevalence of cripples, disease, noise and bad smells. After six months, the eight hundred airwomen residing in Algeria were withdrawn by the WAAF director, who feared that the country was not a good moral influence on her girls! In 1944 the cypherines followed the Mediterranean Area Air Force to Italy, to be joined later by nearly 150 domestic and clerical airwomen, whose task was to keep sections functioning while the RAF men were being demobilised.

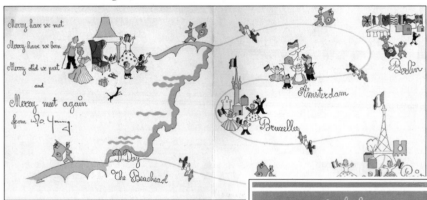

An RAF Christmas card from the 2nd Tactical Air Force, 1944.

The 'Fighting Forty-Five' leave their landing craft at Arromanches, France, on 19th September 1944 (left) and prepare their first camp in an orchard in France (below).

Western Europe

Three WAAF were the first air-ambulance nursing orderlies to set foot in France, seven days after D-Day (June 1944), to begin the evacuation of casualties to Britain. They started a regular shuttle service, which continued as the war progressed.

So many aircraft were commandeered for the Arnhem landings that the first contingent of land-based airwomen – the 'Fighting Forty-Five', the 'cream of the cream' – had to leave by sea for France on 18th September 1944. Their camp was in an orchard with apples falling on their tents and hens clucking outside. From Normandy they flew to Belgium, their number no higher than 260 by December 1944.

The WAAF, supposed to follow their 2nd Tactical Air Force – 85 Group – from Brussels, were delayed by the German breakthrough in the Ardennes. Thus it was not until March 1945 that ten WAAF went to Germany, where some were upset by the ruins of its towns and cities. However, in May 1945 WAAF numbers in western Europe had risen to over 1600 in most trades and branches, and by March 1946 there were WAAF serving in fourteen German stations, as well as in Belgium, France, Holland, Austria and Denmark, with a few also in battle-scarred Malta, the rock of Gibraltar, and nearly two hundred in Italy.

The war ends

VE Day and VJ Day

8th May 1945, the day after the Germans officially surrendered at Rheims, was declared Victory in Europe (VE) Day. Camps celebrated with bonfires (which sometimes got out of hand) and parties. Already the horrors of German concentration camps were known. Prisoners of war were being hastily flown back to airfields to be fed and welcomed by smiling, patient airwomen, and there were tears for those who had died. Now it was 'Burma Looms Ahead' (BLA). This particularly affected WAAF abroad, because the Japanese war continued. Then came the dropping of the atomic bombs and the formal Japanese unconditional surrender on 2nd September, designated Victory over Japan (VJ) Day, with its attendant parades and festivities. At last the Second World War had ended!

A Victory in Europe card, VE Day, 8th May 1945.

Demobilisation

The RAF had already begun Education Vocational Training (EVT) to prepare RAF and WAAF for work after demobilisation. Courses varied from languages to citizenship, housecraft to trade skills. Some WAAF watched displays to advise them on spending their gratuities and clothing coupons (none issued while in the service!). When the war ended, many found their workload either heavier or tailing off. In trades such as plotting and radar, WAAF were found strange new jobs with redundant aircrew. Girls found themselves given a letter and a number for their order in demobilisation. Those married were first out, the single were last. Dates of release were regularly advertised in Air Ministry Orders (AMOs), starting on 18th June 1945.

The day the war ended! The Orderly Room at RAF Andover, Hampshire.

A fashion show in 1945, giving ideas on how to spend discharge money and coupons. Here a WAAF tries on an expensive fur coat, costing more than most could afford.

Below: *Part of the demobilisation process at RAF Wythall, Worcestershire, in 1945.*

After days of clearing from their station and having undergone a medical examination, WAAF leavers went to 105 Dispersal Centre, RAF Wythall, Worcestershire, and joined the long queues of girls snaking around its great hall. There, at different tables, they received clothing coupons, a ration card for food, pay, gratuities, leave passes, £12 10s for the purchase of civilian clothes, unemployment and health insurance cards, their service and release book, and permission to buy 320 cigarettes and 7 ounces (198 grams) of chocolate in the nearby NAAFI. Ten minutes later a WAAF officer shook their hands and thanked them for their service, and then they were out – civilians once again!

Feelings about leaving the WAAF were mixed; the new civilians were afraid and yet excited. They had waited so long for demobilisation and then it had come so quickly. They welcomed their new freedoms: to go home, to leave service restrictions, to wear pretty clothes, to plan their own lives. They were bright with hope. But there were worries about the future – no work, no regular pay, sometimes no home, a hasty marriage, no support from service friends, strangers who would not understand the world they had left behind. The girls had lost their youth but gained confidence and special skills, learnt to adapt and to take the rough with the smooth. 'The WAAF certainly broadened the feet, mind and back', commented one. Several wept for intangibles – routine, security, comradeship. A few remained, and some, finding that civilian life had not changed as they had, later rejoined the WAAF.

A WAAF signing on for the new WRAF, 1st February 1949, Singapore.

Conclusion

The WAAF was intended to keep the RAF flying and to release men for home and overseas duties. At its peak in July 1943 it numbered nearly 182,000 women, comprising 16 per cent of the total RAF strength. WAAF worked in twenty-two officer branches and over eighty trades. During the war about a quarter of a million women had been in the WAAF, and about six hundred women had died while serving. Without their efforts the RAF would have required 150,000 extra men – almost unobtainable.

Although in early days WAAF personnel often had to overcome opposition and hostility, their enthusiasm, conscientiousness and love of the service made its mark. After the war their value was recognised when, on 1st February 1949, they became a permanent service called the Women's Royal Air Force (WRAF), an integral part of the RAF.

Note on dates and names

WRAF	=	1918–20	WRAF	=	1949–94
WAAF	=	1939–49	RAF	=	1994–present

Further reading

Several of the books listed below are out of print but can be obtained through public libraries' inter-library loan systems. There are many small books privately published by individual WAAF on their work during the Second World War, as well as a few novels, which are not included in this list. Most books on the RAF contain references to the WAAF, since it was an integral part of the service; examples include J. Terraine's *Right of the Line* (Hodder & Stoughton, 1985) and M. R. D. Foot's *SOE in France* (HMSO, 1966).

For research, records can be viewed at the National Archives (Ruskin Avenue, Kew, Richmond, Surrey TW9 4DU; telephone: 020 8876 3444; website: www.nationalarchives.gov.uk). Material can also be seen by appointment at the Imperial War Museum (see *Places to visit*), and the RAF Museum, Hendon (see *Places to visit*). The Air Historical Branch (RAF) is due to move in 2008 to a new location; their website can be found at: www.raf.mod.uk – consult History Section). Other contacts are The WAAF Association, website: www.waafassociation.org.uk; The Association of RAF Women Officers, website: www.rafcom.co.uk/support_veterans/wraf.cfm; and a general good RAF website can be found at: www.rafcom.co.uk

The WAAF
Babington-Smith, C. *Evidence in Camera*. David & Charles, 1957.
Beauman, K.B. *Wings on Her Shoulders*. Hutchinson, 1943.
Beauman, K.B. *Partners in Blue*. Hutchinson, 1971.
Clayton, A. *The Enemy Is Listening*. Hutchinson, 1980.
Collett-Wadge, D. *Women in Uniform*. Sampson Low, 1946.
Escott, B.E. *Women in Air Force Blue: 1917–89*. Patrick Stephens, 1989.
Escott, B.E. *Our Wartime Days*. Sutton, 1995.
Hall, A. *We Also Were There*. Merlin Books, 1985.
HEB. *WAAF in Action*. Adam & Charles Black, 1942.
Lucas, Y.M. *WAAF with Wings*. GMS Enterprises, 1992.
Peake, F. *Pure Chance*. Airlife Publishing, 1993.
Pearson, D. *In War and Peace*. Thorogood, 2001.
Portal, Sir Charles, and Forbes, K. J. Trefusis (editors). *Book of the WAAF*. Amalgamated Press, 1942.
Powys-Lybbe, U. *The Eye of Intelligence*. Kimber, 1983.
Smith, M. *Station X*. Channel Four Books, 1998.
Stone, T. *The Integration of Women into Military Service: WAAF in WWII*. Cambridge University Press, 1998.
Warren, P.M. *The Best of Enemies*. Howard Baker, 1986.

SOE
Basu, S. *Spy Princess*. Sutton, 2006.
Binney, M. *The Women Who Lived for Danger*. Hodder & Stoughton, 2002.
Cornioley, P. *Pauline: la vie d'un agent du SOE*. Editions par Exemple, 1996.
Escott, B.E. *Mission Improbable*. Patrick Stephens, 1991.
Escott, B.E. *Twentieth Century Women of Courage*. Sutton, 1999.
Helm, S. *A Life in Secrets*. Little Brown, 2005.
Jones, L. *A Quiet Courage*. Bantam Press, 1990.
Kramer, R. *Flames in the Field*. Michael Joseph, 1995.
Masson, M. *Christine*. Hamish Hamilton, 1975.
Miller, R. *Behind The Lines*. Secker and Warburg, 2002.
Nicholas, E. *Death Be Not Proud*. Cresset Press, 1958.
Overton-Fuller. J. *Noor-un-Nisa Inayat Khan*. Gollancz, 1952.
Walters, A.M. *Moondrop to Gascony*. Macmillan, 1946.

Assistant armourers under training.

Places to visit

Except for the RAF Museum and the Imperial War Museum, actual WAAF material may hardly appear in the museums cited, but a general outline of some aspects of WAAF work or background can be usefully gained. There are many RAF aircraft museums in which occasional WAAF material may appear. Also several closing or closed RAF stations, e.g. Hawkinge, have small museums. Individual county record offices often arrange varied exhibitions, as do small local museums, but none features exclusively WAAF material. It is always advisable to telephone in advance to check opening arrangements and to find out whether the displays you wish to see are accessible.

Bletchley Park, The Mansion, Wilton Avenue, Bletchley, Milton Keynes, Buckinghamshire MK3 6EB. Telephone: 01908 640404. Website: www.bletchleypark.org.uk (Code-breaking and Enigma machine.)

Cabinet War Rooms, Clive Steps, King Charles Street, London SW1A 2AQ (Imperial War Museum). Telephone: 020 7930 6961. Website: www.iwm.org.uk (Churchill's secret underground headquarters.)

Chartwell, Mapleton Road, Westerham, Kent TN16 1PS (National Trust). Telephone: 01732 868381. Website: www.nationaltrust.org.uk (Has material on Churchill and the Second World War.)

D-Day Museum and Overlord Embroidery, Clarence Esplanade, Southsea, Portsmouth, Hampshire PO5 3NT. Telephone: 023 9282 7261.Website: www.ddaymuseum.co.uk

Dover Castle Museum, Market Square, Dover, Kent CT16 1PB (English Heritage). Telephone: 01304 201066. Website: www.dovermuseum.co.uk (Has underground tunnels with displays, including an operations and gun-operations room with WAAF models.)

Eden Camp, Modern History Theme Museum, Malton, North Yorkshire YO17 6RT. Telephone: 01653 697777. Website: www.edencamp.co.uk (WAAF records in store, but available.)

Imperial War Museum, Lambeth Road, London SE1 6HZ. Telephone: 020 7416 5320. Website: www.iwm.org.uk (Includes SOE material, code-breakers, medals, some WAAF/WRAF material and uniforms.)

Imperial War Museum North, The Quays, Trafford Wharf, Trafford Park, Manchester M17 1TZ. Telephone: 0161 836 4000. Website: www.iwm.org.uk (Includes a 'Women in War' exhibition.)

Malvern Museum, The Abbey Gateway, Abbey Road, Great Malvern, Worcestershire WR14 3ES. Telephone: 01684 567811. Website: www.malvernmuseum.co.uk (Includes a small but impressive section on radar.)

National Memorial Arboretum, Croxall Road, Alrewas, Staffordshire DE13 7AR. Telephone: 01283 792333. Website: www.memorialtreesuk.org.uk (Memorials to over 100 military and civilian organisations, including a WAAFA bench and plaque.)

RAF Air Defence Radar Museum, RAF Neatishead, Norwich, Norfolk NR12 8YB. Telephone: 01692 631485. Website: www.radarmuseum.co.uk (Includes a radar system from 1935 and an operations room from 1942.)

Royal Air Force Museum, Grahame Park Way, Hendon, London NW9 5LL. Telephone: 020 8205 2266. Website: www.rafmuseum.org.uk (The best museum for WAAF/WRAF displays.)

Royal Signals Museum, Blandford Camp, Blandford Forum, Dorset DT11 8RH. Telephone: 01258 482248. Website: www.army.mod.uk/royalsignalsmuseum (Mainly has army material but includes some on Enigma and SOE.)

The Second World War Experience Centre, 5 Feast Field (off Town Street), Horsforth, Leeds, West Yorkshire LS18 4TJ. Telephone: 0113 258 4993. Website: www.war-experience.org (Displays some WAAF reference material of constantly changing content.)

Tangmere Museum, Tangmere, Chichester, West Sussex PO20 2ES. Telephone: 01243 790090. Website: www.tangmere-museum.org.uk (This old RAF Battle of Britain fighter station exhibits aircraft as well as SOE and WAAF material.)

Wellesbourne Aviation Museum, Wellesbourne Airfield, Warwick CV35 9JJ. Telephone: 01789 778816. (Very small but has a few WAAF exhibits.)

Yorkshire Air Museum, Airfield Industrial Estate, Halifax Way, Elvington, North Yorkshire YO41 4AU. Telephone: 01904 608595. Website: www.yorkshireairmuseum.co.uk (Has various displays and a memorial garden to WAAF servicewomen.)